she needed a river
/a place to heal her eyes
while washing her ears

J.A.M. Aiwuyor

Our Legaci Press, LLC

Sankofa Mantras:
Positive Words for a Positive Life Grounded in African Wisdom

Copyright © 2018 Jessica Ann Mitchell Aiwuyor

This book or any portion thereof
may not be reproduced or used in any manner whatsoever
without the express written permission of the publisher
except for the use of brief quotations in a book review.

Printed in the United States of America.

First Printing, 2018

ISBN 978-1-948061-03-2

Our Legaci Press, LLC

www.OurLegaciPress.com

Sankofa Mantras

Introduction

The great poet Maya Angelou reminded us that, "Words are things... They get on the walls. They get into your wallpaper. They get in your rugs, in your upholstery, and your clothes, and finally into you." Mantras are a way of using words for this very purpose but in a positive manner. Mantras help us use words in order to speak power, love, and peace into our lives. By using the power of words and allowing specific words to absorb within our thoughts, we can bring a calmness to inner strife - while also working towards mentally, spiritually and physically bringing order to our world.

The hustle and bustle of everyday life often makes us forget the power that we have within ourselves. As we endure everyday needs and struggles, our divine alignment is often unrealized or ignored. We often succumb to feelings of hopelessness or fear. But the truth is, we do have power. We do have the ability to change our world or current circumstance and it all starts with our thoughts. What we tell ourselves matters. The words that we use towards ourselves have an impact. The impact can be positive or negative depending on the words that we use or hear. The words that we absorb affect us every moment of our lives. They affect how we feel about ourselves. They affect our confidence.

In the tradition of African Orature, our ancestors knew this. Our great ancestor Marcus Garvey reminded us, "If you haven't confidence in self, you are twice defeated in the race of life. With confidence, you have won even before you have started."

When our ancestors endured chattel slavery, colonialism, Jim Crow and apartheid, they used the power of freedom songs to keep going. Some of the key leaders of slave rebellions were preachers, mostly due to their ability to read and use the words of the Bible in order to envision the freedom and liberation of their people.

Those of our ancestors that could not read or write used the power of Negro Spirituals to help them make it through hard work days as a tool for survival. They sang these spirituals over and over again for hundreds of years. I am convinced that we have yet to fully realize the strength and power in the words of those songs. These same spirituals like," Go down Moses," "Wade in the water," and "Follow the drinking gourd," were used as word guides for runaway slaves escaping to freedom. Later, we used the power of spoken word and freedom songs in the civil rights, freedom fighter, anti-colonialism, and anti-apartheid movements.

All of this is directly connected to the emphasis on spoken word throughout African oral traditions. Many Western African societies had seers and griots that preserved our stories and carried generations of history through their performances. These performances were used to entertain, inform, and inspire. Indeed, Black people have a long and ancient history that thrives on the energy of the spoken word. Sankofa Mantras follows the resilient path of our ancestors that used spoken word to sustain life and eventually get free. Though we may not be in the same type of bondage that many of our ancestors endured, we often face daily struggles that weigh heavily on our souls. In these circumstances, it is important to remember that the roadmap has been laid out before us. We have liberated ourselves before and can always do it again. This liberation can be physical, but also mental and spiritual. Sankofa Mantras serves as a reminder that freedom, though hard fought, is possible - with trust in ourselves, the guidance of our ancestors and most of all faith in God.

Sankofa Mantras features a series of 100 powerful affirmations based on ancient West African symbols. Adinkra symbols, from the Akan people of Ghana and Côte d'Ivoire, are widely known for their special wisdom and knowledge. Adinkra symbols are often printed in patterns on cloth and worn for funeral rites and other important events[1].

---

[1] W. Bruce Willis, *The Adinkra dictionary: A visual primer on the language of Adinkra*, (Pyramid Complex 1998)

The symbols are used as a form of communication and for their spiritual meanings, connected with cultural proverbs.[2]

Adinkra symbols have become a source of wisdom and cultural pride for the African Diaspora (the descendants of enslaved Africans brought to the Americas during the Trans-Atlantic Slave Trade). In fact, many of the enslaved Africans brought to the Americas were Akan people. In recent years, Adinkra symbols have become more prevalent among African Americans, Afro-Latinos, Afro-Caribbean people and other children of the Diaspora as many seek to heal and reconnect with our African roots.

Each affirmation applies the powerful guidance of 11 Adinkra symbols towards embracing peace, self-love, knowledge, and faith. The mantras can be read at home in a peaceful setting. They can also be read when traveling on the bus or train, on the way to work, and during lunch breaks. Repeatedly read the mantras that speak to you the most. When you are at home, try reading them out loud. Write the ones that speak the most to you on sticky notes and post them on your mirrors or windows. You might have seen the popular TV character, "Mary Jane Pollard," do this on the hit BET show "Being Mary Jane." Well, this a real practice that is very helpful for keeping thoughts centered because it keeps our words of encouragement in constant view.

Also, I strongly encourage you to create your own mantras that apply specifically to your life. There are pages available at the end of this book for you to start writing your own mantras. No one knows your story and what you need to hear better than yourself. Take some quiet time to listen to your spirit. Write down what comes to you. Let your feelings pour out. Write a mantra or poem for your life that you can use on a daily basis. This can be in any form. Mine are usually poems or free verses. Use the power of your own words and creativity to speak new energy into your life.

---

[2] G. F. Kojo Arthur, *Cloth As Metaphor: (Re)reading the Adinkra Cloth: Symbols of the Akan of Ghana, 2nd Edition (iUniverse, 2017)*, 11, 16-17.

The affirmations within Sankofa Mantras are stepping stones for helping you on the journey of self-realization, confidence, and self-love. Trust and believe in yourself. And always remember, "We've come this far by faith."

Sankofa

"Go back and get it."

The Sankofa Bird symbolizes the need to use our cultural legacy, along with lessons from the past in order to move forward.

Remembering

the triumphs of

my ancestors,

I know that

I can survive

any challenge

before me.

I will look back

to walk

forward.

I will use past

struggles

as motivation.

I embrace

my

authentic self.

I will look

within

for guidance.

I will look

within

for peace.

I

celebrate

my past

my future

AND

my right now.

I am

unstoppable.

Generations

of

perseverance

are on

my side.

I am never

alone.

My

mothers and fathers

before me

are

always with

me.

I will

honor

the dreams

of my ancestors

by respecting

all opportunities

given to me.

I

honor

my

story.

I

value

my truth.

Akoma

"A heart."

Akoma represents the heart and the need for us to operate from a place of love and patience.

I will be kind

to

my spirit.

I will be

gentle

with my

soul.

Love sustains life.

I love myself

continually

and

without

judgment.

I will nourish my

body with healthy foods.

I will nourish my

mind with healthy thoughts.

I will nourish

my soul with healthy love.

I

boldly

love

my

authentic self.

I

choose

me.

The universe

propels me

to do

great things.

I welcome

this truth with my

whole heart

and mind.

I will

speak from

love

or

not at all.

I walk in light.

Speak in love.

Live in peace.

I

embrace

others

with

a

pure heart

and

open mind.

Like a heart that

curves

within,

I

accept me.

I love myself.

I value

my uniqueness.

I deserve:

Respect

Love

Care

Happiness

Prosperity

Understanding

With time,

I will rise

to

great heights.

With self-love,

I will rise

to great

peace.

Like an oak tree seedling,

with patience

I will grow.

And once

I have

grown,

it will be hard for

me

to fall.

I celebrate

my

achievements.

Day by day.

Week by week.

Year by year.

I

embrace

my entire

self

with

love and courage.

Gye Nyame

"Only God."

Gye Nyame symbolizes the supremacy of God throughout our lives.

I welcome God's presence.

I welcome peace.

I welcome courage.

I welcome understanding.

I welcome protection.

I welcome clarity.

I can

accomplish

any goal

when I walk

in my

divine purpose.

I am God's child.

I honor

and

love myself.

I only

accept respect

from others.

With

God

on my side,

fear is unnecessary

stress.

Today,

I love myself,

just as I am,

knowing that

I am made

in the image

of my creator.

No matter what I've been through,

No one can alter my path.

No one can change my purpose.

No one has that power over me.

No one has that power over my life

but God.

I welcome God's presence.

I welcome divine peace.

I welcome divine courage.

I welcome divine understanding.

I welcome divine protection.

Akofena

"War sword."

Akofena is a symbol of two swords crossed, representing courage and responsibility.

I break the

shackles of doubt.

I embrace

confidence.

I invite

clarity.

I move forward

with intent,

authority,

and without

permission.

I am

a

courageous

being

in control

of my soul.

I will fight for

my life.

I will

fight for

my freedom.

What others think of me

is not my priority.

_____

My life is my priority.

Fulfilling my purpose is my priority.

Making a positive impact

on the world is my priority.

My strength and well being

are my priorities.

In every

circumstance

my life

is my own.

My soul is free

from the weight

of others.

My life,

my health,

my joy,

are God-given rights.

_____

I am vigilant

in

protecting

them.

I am already

victorious

because

I

have

survived.

My enemies tried but cannot destroy me.

I am blessed.

I am strengthened.

I am rising

and now

emboldened.

In every circumstance,

I will trust myself.

In all situations,

I will listen to my soul.

I will protect my spirit.

I am still here.

I am still here.

I

am

still

here.

Ashe'

Nea Onnim No Sua A Ohu

"He who does not know, will know after learning."

Nea Onnim represents on-going growth through learning and education.

I will

not

crumble.

Every day

from my past

lights

the path

towards my future.

My story

has

strength.

My experiences

give me the power

to overcome

any circumstance.

Every mistake

provides gained

knowledge.

Every loss

provides

a lesson

learned.

I still have time.

I welcome

each day moving

forward,

knowing that

I have another

chance.

My intuition

is my soul

guiding my path.

I will listen.

I will listen.

I will listen.

I celebrate

my life.

I celebrate

my growth.

I recognize

every

challenge

as an

opportunity

to blossom.

I

let go

of the

pain

and

I embrace

the lesson.

I will

expand

my mind

by feeding

it

wise words.

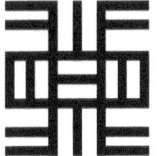

Dwennimmen

"Ram's horns."

Dwennimmen symbolizes the need to be strong but also humble.

I will listen to the voice that says, "Stop."

I will listen to the voice that says, "Wait."

I will allow myself room to grow.

I will give myself space to rise.

And when it is time to fly,

I will go.

My inner voice

is my

soul speaking.

I am

both

conscious and confident.

I am saved

by

embracing

my truth.

My imperfections

are tools

helping to

guide my

divine purpose.

I am both imperfect AND worthy.

Nyame Nti

"By God's grace."

Nyame Nti depicts a growing crop. It symbolizes the trust and faith that God will provide for our needs.

I am

surrounded

by thousands

of daily blessings

and miracles.

I embrace

my purpose

and trust

in

God.

Anything

I

need

will

be

provided.

I will prosper,

even in deserts.

My roots are

watered

wherever I go.

Joy comes not only in the morning.

Joy comes by moonlight.

Joy comes through winds.

Joy comes through rains.

I accept the unpredictability of life,

knowing that

even through hard times

I am favored.

I am filled with power.

I am showered with grace.

I will use both

to overcome all battles.

With endurance,

I will

expand.

With faith,

I will

conquer.

I am like

a

resilient

flower.

When the wind blows,

I don't crumble.

I populate.

I will

persevere.

I will persist.

I will thrive.

"Trouble don't last always."

Like the sun

behind clouds,

I shine continually

and

I am

continually blessed.

My path is cleared.

My steps are ordered.

I am

whole.

I am

healed.

I am

free.

Peace

covers me

like a

blanket

of snow.

I deserve

to be here.

Just as

I am.

I will lean on faith.

I will trust in God.

I am thankful for my life.

I am thankful for my past.

I am thankful for my journey.

I am thankful

for

every day,

every moment,

and

every blessing.

Bese Saka

"Cluster of cola nuts."

Bese Saka symbolizes abundance, affluence, and power.

My soul is more

valuable

than

what the material

world has to offer.

The universe

supports

me in

all of

my

ambitions.

I am victorious.

I am prosperous.

I am abundant.

My gifts are divine.

I will use them

accordingly.

I trust my talents.

I trust my passions.

They are

powerfully

aligned

with my purpose.

I am surrounded by light.

I am filled with light.

Glowing

is my

natural state

of

being.

The source.

The light.

The truth,

are all

within

me.

I will act accordingly.

My life

is

plentiful.

My world

is

abundant.

I prosper in all stages of life.

When it feels like I'm losing,
I'm learning.

When it feels like I'm struggling,
I'm training.

When it feels like I'm dormant,
I'm planning.

When it feels like I'm down,
I'm resting.

When it feels like I'm up,
I'm shining.

I invite confidence.

I invite time.

I invite order.

I invite space.

I invite faith.

I invite prosperity.

I invite success.

I invite bliss.

I invite peace.

I invite love.

I invite health.

I invite the wealth and happiness of life.

I am valuable.

I am worthy.

I recognize the powers

I have within.

Ananse Ntontan

"The spider's web."

Ananse Ntontan symbolizes wisdom, creativity, and life's complexities.

I uplift my creativity.

I uplift my power

to

shape and shift

the world

before me.

I am

a

creative being.

I will honor

my gifts

by using

them wisely.

With my own vision,

    I mold my world.

With my own heart,

    I shape my now.

With my own hands,

    I build my future.

With my mind,

with my skills,

with my hopes,

with my dreams,

I will make

a way out of

no way

by creating

a new way.

With my mind,

I image.

With my mouth,

I form.

With my hands,

I build.

With my creativity,

I mold the world before me.

I am pure energy.

Renewed

&

Renewed

&

Renewed again.

Sesa Wo Suban

"Transform your life."

Sesa Wo Suban is two symbols joined together. The "Morning Star" represents new beginnings. The wheel represents movement.

Like a caterpillar

in its cocoon,

I honor my ability

to

radically transform

and

soar

in due time.

I emerge from

every challenge,

transformed

by knowledge

and strengthened

by wisdom.

Like the dung beetle

in ancient sands,

I withstand hard winds.

I emerge from long nights

renewed,

reborn,

and

stronger.

With faith,

I will push through

what is before me and step into a greater path.

It is never too late.

It is never too late.

It is never too late,

to choose a new path

and embrace my calling.

My spirit rises with every new dawn.

I can and will

change

my current circumstance.

I can and will

move forward

in a better, greater

direction.

Duafe

"Wooden comb."

Duafe symbolizes all things beautiful and pure.

Like the water

of rivers,

I am

on a

wondrous journey.

Beautiful.

Spontaneous. Purposeful.

Like a

blossoming flower,

my

beauty

grows

within.

I am at peace with my true self.

The self without makeup.

The self without expensive clothing.

The self without outside approval.

The self without outside acceptance.

I am at peace with me.

Born as I am,

already

complete, worthy, and, free.

I must speak my truth.

I must live my life,

freely and fully.

I choose life.

I choose this day

to follow

my path.

My journey is my own.

There is no

need

to

compare.

I absorb the beauty of life,

I command the power of my soul.

I transcend all confusion and strife.

My soul is at peace.

My mind is at ease.

My spirit is cleansed.

Self Care

Accompany your use of mantras with the following self-care activities to relieve stress and develop your inner growth. All of the following activities are suggestions that have helped many people from all walks of life. However, these suggestions are not intended to replace the guidance of a mental health professional or medical physician.

Start journaling.

Write down your thoughts as a form of release or start writing your goals and dreams. Take time to reflect on your life. Think about how you feel right now. Think about your accomplishments - big or small.

Have tea time.

Brew homemade tea in a pot over the stove. Mix ingredients that bring joy to your taste buds and warm the soul. The ingredients could include cinnamon sticks, citrus peels, or mint leaves. Allow the aroma to fill the room. Drink the tea quietly while reflecting, journaling or reading a book.

Exercise.

Get moving according to your abilities. Find a way to sweat. This can be through jogging, walking, or cardio workouts.

Eat fresh.

Cut up some apples, bananas, mangoes or any other fruits that are near you. Eat them while drinking a large cup of water. Wash down impurities and nourish your body simultaneously.

Hydrate.

We absorb so many impurities in the hustle and bustle of life. Sometimes it's good to consciously flush them out and rehydrate your body. A good way of doing this is by increasing the amount of water we drink. Take seven days to intentionally drink water instead of sodas, juice, alcohol, and other drinks.

Meditate.

Take time to clear your thoughts. You can do this by sitting in silence and reflecting. You can pick a soothing mantra to repeat out loud or to yourself. You can also listen to calming music or sounds, like the sound of rain or the ocean. Research the different forms of meditation and if possible get a meditation guide to help you through the process.

Rock out.

Play some of your favorite songs and dance until you sweat. Dance until your soul feels satisfied. Dance until you've shaken off all negativity and shaken on power and joy.

Declutter.

Depending on where you live or your lifestyle, you may find yourself surrounded by extra things that not only take up the physical space around you but also clutters your mental and spiritual space - often unknowingly. People that have taken time to declutter often feel lighter, like a weight has been lifted off of their shoulders.

Take some time to observe your environment. Is it cluttered? If yes, this may be an opportunity to cleanse your space and donate to a local thrift store or someone in need.

Get a checkup.

Not everyone has access to quality healthcare. However, if you do have healthcare, I strongly encourage you to get regular checkups. Our health is a blessing that we often take for granted.

Go to counseling.

Sometimes it's hard for us to admit that we need additional help on our self-care journey. This is especially considering the fact that help may be difficult to get. However, if you are dealing with an issue traumatic or otherwise, I strongly suggest speaking with a therapist. They can help you work through your thoughts and provide you with additional medical assistance if needed.

When my younger brother passed away, I knew it was a difficult situation. I knew that *Sankofa* would guide me but I also knew that I needed to speak with someone to help me through the grief process. Speaking with a therapist helped me work towards healing.

Never underestimate the power of speaking and writing for growth and healing.

Listen to yourself.

Think of other activities that make you feel free and whole. Make a list and try to incorporate them into your daily habits.

Journal

As I stated earlier, it is always a good idea to write down your thoughts. Give your mind a release by writing out your feelings, wants, needs, prayers, mantras, poems, goals, and anything else that you've been holding in. Always remember the power within you. When all else fails, let the essence of Sankofa lead the way.

This journal is a starting point that you can use to express yourself. Don't hold back. Write what is true to you. You never know what you've been holding on to. If you feel stuck. Re-read the mantras that you connect with the most. Use them as a guide and let the writing flow from there.

www.ingramcontent.com/pod-product-compliance
Lightning Source LLC
Chambersburg PA
CBHW030153100526
44592CB00009B/261